TRANSFORMATION

TRANSFORMATION

• • • • • • • • • • • • •

A 13-SESSION SMALL GROUP EXPLORATION
VIA DIALOG OF THE GOSPEL ACCORDING TO JOHN

BASED ON THE BOOK, *THE TRANSFORMATION*, WRITTEN BY
JOHN DANNEMILLER AND IRVING STUBBS

ADAPTED FOR USE BY SMALL GROUPS BY
BRIAN REGRUT

Transformation
© 2021 Living Dialog Ministries
PO Box 15125
Richmond, VA 23227

All Rights Reserved

Published in the United States of America by Living Dialog Ministries, a 501(c)(3) tax exempt organization. www.livingdialog.org

ISBN 978 0 9890791-4-3

Scripture quotations, unless otherwise indicated, are taken from the HOLY BIBLE NEW INTERNATIONAL VERSION. Copyright © 1973, 1978, 1984, 2011 by International Bible Society. Used by permission of Zondervan. All rights reserved.

Cover and interior design by Frank Gutbrod

18 17 16 15 14 13 7 6 5 4 3 2 1

Printed in the United States of America

CONTENTS

INTRODUCTION *07*

SESSION 1: Why is Jesus referred to as The Word? *12*

SESSION 2: Who is John the Baptizer? *17*

SESSION 3: What did Jesus do and say? *22*

SESSION 4: Why did Jesus meet with society's outcasts? *30*

SESSION 5: Why is it hard to understand some of Jesus' teachings? *38*

SESSION 6: What does it mean to be a Slave of Sin? *46*

SESSION 7: Why does Jesus identify as a shepherd? *56*

SESSION 8: What does Jesus want his followers to understand? *63*

SESSION 9: What does Jesus mean when he says, "I have overcome the world"? *69*

SESSION 10: How did Jesus spend his last hours with the disciples? *77*

SESSION 11: Why did Jesus have to die? *83*

SESSION 12: How did Jesus' closest followers react to the resurrection? *92*

SESSION 13: What does Transformation look like? *97*

EPILOGUE *103*

INTRODUCTION

We've designed this 13-session study to help small groups engage in dialog about Jesus, the most important individual in world history. During this study we'll encourage exploration of the fundamentals of the Christian life, as we listen to the teachings of Jesus and see how he interacted with the people from all walks of life.

Our hope is that as you read the scripture, wrestle with the questions, and listen to what others are discovering, you will gain a richer understanding of Jesus and what it means to be transformed into a Child of God. Rich in theology, and essential to evangelism, this study offers a new and refreshing guide to The Gospel According to the Apostle John. If you have questions about what you've heard about Jesus or if you have questions you'd like to ask him, you will find these weekly moments of study exceptionally interesting.

We'll be getting to know Jesus better and learn how to relate to one another through transforming conversations and discussions. Despite the benefits that many experience through modern communication systems, most of our day-to-day messaging is relatively superficial. Most of the global population is conditioned to skim along the surface of ideas and events without discovering the profound truths that lie deep inside them.

Truthfully, experiences are richer when they're shared. If you experienced a miraculous life event or experience and saw things you'd never seen before, wouldn't you want to tell someone about it? Better yet, wouldn't you like to have someone along to share the "Wow!"?

In your assembly of companions journeying through Jesus' messages and meanings, you are invited to share your experiences through dialog. We believe the meaning of the word "dialog" is a "big" talk, a heart-to-heart sharing that has the power to transform everyone participating in the conversation. Our goal is simple. When you read this, our hope and prayer is: "You will know Jesus as you've never known him before."

Kinds of dialogs

There are different kinds of dialogs we'll experience during our gatherings:

- *Dialog with God* — We believe that God calls each of us to a relationship with him. This relationship gives meaning and purpose to our lives. God wants deep, personal, and open communication with us.

- *Dialog with self* — As you eavesdrop on Jesus' conversations and spy on the events of his life, you may have thoughts and feelings that clarify, stretch, and challenge your understanding of Jesus. You may think, "Did he really say that?", "I wonder what he meant by that?" or "I never thought about it that way before."

- *Dialog with others who are physically present* — The exchange of thoughts and feelings amplify and deepen your understanding. Some of us learn of Jesus from the word of others.

- *Dialog with others who aren't present* — The words and ideas of others you've known interact with your own thoughts and shape your perceptions in both positive and negative ways.

Invitation to dialog

The kind of dialog we want to cultivate in our group is not another word for "discussion" or "debate". Discussion is analytical and typically picks things apart. In debate, sides work to win points. Dialog, on the other hand, is a way for us together to seek understanding.

Dialog is intended to:
- not to advocate but inquire
- not to argue but explore
- not to convince but discover

We listen to one another to find out what is meant. We assume each member of the group has a piece of the answer to the question, and that together, the group can craft a new and better answer. We celebrate new insights, greater clarity, and deeper understandings when they occur.

Agreement is not the purpose of dialog. It is important to suspend judgment about others' contributions. Disagreements can be seen as a different way of looking at a subject. Disagreements can energize a group to seek meaning and clarity that goes beyond initial conflicting views.

How to use this guide

The thirteen sessions in this guide will guide your group in dialog with Jesus and with one another through Christ's powerful messages.

This guide couldn't be simpler to use. No advance preparation or study is required! Some groups may choose to begin each gathering with prayer, or take a few minutes to catch up on one another's lives.

To launch into your time of dialog, your facilitator or someone from your group will read a few brief paragraphs that are a mix of summary and direct quotations from the Bible. Immediately following each section, you'll find a question or two designed to launch your group into dialog over the events and issues raised in the text. Your group should stop at the end of each segment to consider the questions that are posed before moving onto the next segment of text. The questions will look like this:

> Are you open to experiencing a spiritual transformation? Why or why not?

You'll find additional questions at the end of each session if your group is looking for further discussion for personal reflection.

Plan on an hour or so for dialog for each meeting. Some groups have gone far beyond an hour due to the intensity and enjoyment of the dialog. Your group's facilitator should be sensitive to the time commitment each member has made to the group. Make sure those in the group agree to go beyond the stated time if extended discussion time seems to be warranted.

Remember that your group's facilitator is there not as an answer man or woman, but as a coach. Each member of your group brings insight and value to the dialog as you craft an answer together. Your facilitator will help to honor your group's time commitment and guide you through the material each week.

You'll close each session with dialog in prayer. Affirming that Christ has been with you as you've shared a meal and talked about his story each week is the foundation for this time. Members of your group may have needs in their lives or questions and concerns raised through the session's dialog. This guide offers some general tips about how to pray conversationally, as well as suggestions for how to shape your prayer experience. Prayer may not be a familiar discipline to you — but it can be as simple as dialoguing with a friend. And you are!

Each person must make his or her own decision whether to become a follower of Jesus or not. This decision has eternal implications. We hope and pray that you and your group enjoy your journey together alongside Jesus with John as your guide. May each member be blessed, challenged, and encouraged as you consider his words for becoming a new creation in Christ, transformed. Ok, let's get started.

SESSION 1

WHY IS JESUS REFERRED TO AS THE WORD?
John 1:1–18

We are about to embark on one of the most rewarding of all studies of God's Word. As you will see, The Gospel According to the Apostle John is unique among the four gospels. In the Book of John, we see more of the human side of Jesus than we see in any of the four gospel accounts. Remember, Jesus was both fully God and fully man, a divine concept around which it is difficult for us to wrap our human minds. Even so, John, inspired by the Holy Spirit, shows us a Jesus with whom we can easily relate. He gets angry, he weeps in shared sorrow and he suffers in spirit and in body in much the same way we experience these aspects of life. So prepare your hearts for a unique view of a unique individual, for there has never before been nor will there ever be again, One who is like our Savior, Jesus Christ.

In this session we will look at an introduction to John's gospel that challenges us to see Christ through a different spiritual lens. In Session Two we will study the remainder of the first chapter to better understand the role of John the Baptizer and the calling of the men who will be Jesus' closest companions for the following three years.

The Bible's New Testament begins with the four gospels, each provided by a different writer and each similar to the others in various ways. The gospels are dissimilar in that each is written for a different audience and offers the perspective of the author. Matthew, Mark, and Luke, are narratives of the life, teachings, and works of Jesus. John's gospel, by contrast, is written to clearly affirm that Jesus is the Christ, the son of God, and that by believing we may have life in his name.

Unlike the gospels of Matthew and Luke, John does not begin his account with the nativity. Rather than beginning with Jesus' birth or with the beginning of his ministry, John goes back to before time, to a place where there existed only God, the Father, the Son, and the Holy Spirit. The Apostle John begins at the VERY beginning. He initiates his gospel with, *"In the beginning was the Word, and the Word was with God, and the Word was God. He was with God in the beginning."* (John 1:1) And so begins a unique journey through the life, death, and resurrection of Jesus Christ, a journey which shows us Christ's humanity as well as his divinity.

John's launch of his Gospel sounds a great deal like a poem or even a song lyric. His reference to Jesus, the Christ, as the Word may have sounded similar to Greek philosophy to early readers and may have been intended to draw the attention of Jew and Gentile alike. For whatever reason the Holy Spirit inspired John to begin in this manner, we do know that he begins early in his gospel account to present the story of Jesus' life in a unique way.

For instance, rather than referring to himself in the first, or second person, John would refer to himself at least six times in his gospel in the third person as "the disciple whom Jesus loved." We can only speculate his reasoning for writing in this manner but many believe that John wished to divert attention away from his own name in favor of the name of Jesus Christ. Perhaps, in his humility, he saw himself as being unnecessary. Thus, he seldom used his own name.

However, by referring to himself as "the disciple whom Jesus loved" John reveals something about his gospel account that is undeniable; John was presenting us with a far more personal picture of Jesus than any of the other gospels.

It is on Christ as the Living Word of God that John places his emphasis in the first part of Chapter 1. Inspired by the Holy Spirit, John saw Jesus as more than one who would *speak* the Word. John saw Jesus as the Living, Breathing Word of the Father who came down from heaven to have fellowship with mankind.

[John:1:1,2]

- Someone stated that "from the begingless beginning" there has been God. What do you think that means?
- John tells us that, "The Word was with God, and the Word was God." (John 1:1) Explain how this is true.

John then details the work of the Word.
- All things were made through him
- Life was in him, and that life was the light of humanity
- That light shines in the darkness
- The darkness has not understood that light

When Jesus was born in the flesh, over 400 years had passed since Israel had heard from God through a prophet (Haggai, Zachariah and Malachi). The Jews had languished under the rule and sometimes under the oppression of Gentile kingdoms. They had been subjugated by the Babylonians, the Medo-Persians, the Greeks and, when Jesus was born, they were under the iron rule of the Romans. Israel longed for the prophesied messiah to come and set them free and reestablish the Kingdom of Israel, restoring the "glory days" of King David and King Solomon.

In this first section of John's gospel, he speaks of a world of darkness into which "the Light" has come. This bears a striking resemblance to the messianic prophecy found in Isaiah 9:2 "The people walking in darkness have seen a great light". Truly, Jesus did come to all mankind. However, John reveals to us a Christ who comes into the heart of every individual believer. In fact, John bears witness to Jesus' power to **TRANSFORM** the individual when he states, *"to those who believed in His name, he gave the right to become (be transformed into) children of God"*

[John 1:3–12]

> ■ **What do you think John means when he refers to "the darkness" in which "the Light" shines?**

John ends his introduction to his gospel with *"The Word became flesh and made his dwelling among us. We have seen his glory, the glory of the one and only Son, who came from the Father, full of grace and truth."*

[John 1:14]

FOR FURTHER DISCUSSION OR PERSONAL REFLECTION:

[JOHN 1:1]

The book of Genesis, like the book of John starts with the words, "In the beginning . . ." How are these two introductions similar? How do they differ?

[JOHN 1:1-18]

John opens his gospel with his perception of God in Jesus as Word and Light and Life. What is your perception of God? What do you liken him to?

[JOHN 1:12-14]

What does it mean to become a child of God? How can this be accomplished?

SESSION 2

WHO IS JOHN THE BAPTIZER?
John 1:19-51

As we move away from John's introduction we will now learn about the one who was chosen to prepare the way for Jesus and we will see the beginning of the process Jesus employs of assembling the 12 men who would be his constant companions for more than three years.

After establishing Jesus as the incarnate Word of God, John moves on to the beginning of Christ's earthly ministry. He lays the groundwork for this by once again mentioning the fulfillment of prophecy.

Isaiah spoke of one to come who would be "the voice of one calling in the wilderness: *'Prepare the way for the Lord.'*" (Isaiah 40:3). This was to be the role that John the Baptizer would fulfill and it would be the mission that he would confess when confronted by the Pharisees who were prominent religious leaders of the nation of Israel. The Baptizer readily admitted that he was not the Messiah who was to redeem Israel but that he was simply to prepare the way for the Messiah by preaching a doctrine of repentance. The religious leaders, called Pharisees, had issues even with this message but they would not attempt to harm John because they knew that the people considered him a prophet.

John the Baptizer is an interesting character study. He knew he was not to become the "main attraction" but he was content to fulfill the role that God had set for him. The Baptizer's greatest words were regarding the Messiah whose way he prepared. For instance, when he said, *"Look, the Lamb of God, who takes away the sin of the world!"* he was fulfilling his role as the forerunner by directing attention away from himself and toward Jesus.

[John 1:18–28]

> - What did the prophet Isaiah mean when he spoke of John saying that he would "prepare the way for the Lord"?
> - Do you think that you would have had a hard time fulfilling the role of John the Baptizer, knowing that Jesus would be getting all the glory even though John had prepared the way?

The next day, John would baptize the Son of God and later make his dramatic testimony, referring to when he baptized Jesus, saying, "I saw the Spirit come down from heaven as a dove and remain on him. And I myself did not know him, but the one who sent me to baptize with water told me, *'The man on whom you see the Spirit come down and remain is the one who will be baptized with the Holy Spirit. I have seen and I testify,'* he said, *'that this is God's chosen one.'"* It was after this that Jesus would go into the wilderness to prepare for the full coming of his earthly ministry.

In the third chapter of John's gospel, Jesus quoted the baptizer as saying, *"He (the Messiah) must become greater; I must become less"* (John 3:30) John is a perfect example of how we all have a role to play in God's great plan and it is in fulfilling this role that we find life's greatest contentment.

[John 1:29-34]

> John the baptizer knew his role and his mission in God's great plan. Do you know your role in God's plan and if not, how do you find out what that your role is to be?

John the Baptizer had many disciples who followed him, listening to his teachings. It was one of these disciples, named Andrew, who would hear this John proclaim that Jesus was the *"Lamb of God"*. In response, Andrew chose to follow Jesus. He went and got his brother Simon and told him, *"We have found the Messiah (that is the Christ)."* Simon would then become a disciple of Christ and Jesus would give Simon the name Cephas, which means Peter (the Greek word for rock).

The next day Jesus invited a man named Philip to follow him. Philip found Nathaniel and told him, *"We have found the one Moses wrote about in the Law, and about whom the prophets also wrote—Jesus of Nazareth, the son of Joseph."* Nathaniel responded by asking if anything good could come from Nazareth. Philip responded cryptically, *"Come and see."*

When he met Nathaniel, Jesus said some things that suggested that he already knew the man. Nathaniel's response was a remarkable shift from his earlier skepticism. *"Rabbi,"* he said, *"you are the Son of God; you are the King of Israel."*

Jesus then told him: *"You believe because I told you I saw you under the fig tree. You shall see greater things . . . You will see heaven open, and the angels of God ascending and descending on the Son of Man."*

[John 1:35–51]

> ■ **Nathaniel believed in Jesus as the Christ largely because of a miraculous revelation which Christ shared with him. Do you believe that such revelations still occur today? Why or why not?**

John's gospel does not record the calling of all twelve of his disciples. John doesn't even mention his own calling. In this passage, only Andrew, Phillip, Peter and Nathaniel are specifically mentioned. However, as we move forward through the following chapters we find that Jesus had called the twelve and that they had set out on Jesus' mission of redeeming mankind from sin.

FOR FURTHER DISCUSSION OR PERSONAL REFLECTION:

[JOHN 1:29-34]

What great revelation did John the Baptistizer receive from God?

When John the Baptistizer saw Jesus approaching the river, he called him *"the Lamb of God"*. What did this mean?

[JOHN 1:35-50]

Who was the first disciple Jesus called and how did his call create a domino effect? How does this become a pattern for us to follow in sharing Christ with others?

Why did Jesus need a team of disciples?

SESSION 3

WHAT DID JESUS DO AND SAY?

John 2:1–3:36

Chapters 2 and 3 offer us a greater understanding of the work in Jesus' life of the Holy Spirit and of the Father than in any of the gospels. The Holy Spirit was more than a concept to Jesus. Christ was in such harmony of purpose and consistency of contact with the Father and the Holy Spirit that he clearly portrayed his later claim in John 14 that *"the Father and I are One."* It is now through his relationship with the Father and the power of the Holy Spirit that Jesus performs the first of his many miracles. And it is through the same singularity of purpose and person that we are presented with the opportunity to experience the greatest of all experiences, that of being spiritually born again.

I n this Gospel, our early views of Jesus are dramatic. The first of his public miraculous signs was changing water into wine at a wedding in Cana of Galilee. Wedding feasts in Jesus' day lasted seven days with people coming and going as their schedules allowed and the wine was known to flow freely. In this wedding something embarrassing happened: the supply of wine ran out. After Jesus' mother encouraged him to offer a helping hand, Jesus transformed the water in six 30-gallon jars into wine. The master of the banquet declared the new wine to be the choice wine of the feast. John tells us that Jesus did this to reveal his glory as a result, his disciples believed in him.

Arthur John Gossip speaks with winsome eloquence about what this meant. He says that the main lesson of this event "is the glory that Christ brings with him—a life that is abundant life, a peace that passes understanding, a fullness of joy that only he can give, and that produces an astonishment in its recipients like the steward of the feast. That", adds Gossip, "is the characteristic note of the New Testament. Always its people keep bursting in on us, their eyes shining, their hearts on fire, crying, 'We've found it!' The thing for which the whole world has been seeking, and it works!" (1952).

[John 2:1–12]

- **Jesus changed the water into wine at the urging of his mother. Why do you think that she took it upon herself to urge Jesus into public ministry and was this timing right?**
- **Why was the wine that Jesus created from water better than the "best" wine provided for the guests at the beginning of the feast?today. What do you think accounts for the differences?**
- **In what way did this event "reveal his (Christ's) glory"?**

When it was almost time for the Jewish Passover, Jesus and his disciples went to Jerusalem. It is at this point in John's gospel that we are told about Jesus driving the moneychangers out of the temple. They found vendors in the temple courts selling animals for burnt offerings and exchanging money for the currency required to pay the temple tax. The implication is that the moneychangers were exacting an unfair fee from those who exchanged their currency. Jesus drove them out of the temple area, scattered the moneychangers' coins, and said, *"Stop turning my Father's house into a market!"*

The temple courts were the outer precincts of the temple that Gentiles, as well as Jews, were permitted to enter. The animals offered for sacrifice had to pass inspection to ensure that they were blemish-free. The moneychangers exchanged the Roman coins that temple visitors brought for the Tyrian shekels required for the annual tax payment to the temple treasury. Jewish leaders challenged Jesus on his authority to take these steps, demanding that Jesus perform a miracle to validate his claims of authority.

Jesus responded: *"Destroy this temple, and I will raise it again in three days."*

His challengers noted that it took 46 years to build the temple. John reminds us that the temple to which Jesus referred was his own body and not the temple building and that Jesus was foretelling his own resurrection from the dead three days after his crucifixion.

John records this event as happening at the beginning of Jesus' ministry while the other gospels record it much later. Most Bible scholars believe that the seeming discrepancy is easily explained by the fact that Jesus attended more than one Passover in Jerusalem and that similar events happened on two separate occasions. This visit came early in Jesus' ministry while the other visit, referred to in the other gospels, took place only days prior to Christ's crucifixion.

Many were impressed with these signs and believed in his name. "But Jesus would not entrust himself to them, for he knew all people. He did not need any testimony about mankind, for he knew what was in each person."

[John 2:13–25]

> - What current examples of the commercialization of religion or religious institutions can you think of that might compare to the presence of vendors in the temple in Jesus' day?
>
> - If you were a reporter for a *Jerusalem News Agency* and were present for the cleansing of the temple, how would you report the incident? What headline would you give for your article?

Joshua Hammer captures the history of the Temple Mount. "Jewish tradition holds that it is the site where God gathered the dust to create Adam and where Abraham nearly sacrificed his son Isaac to prove his faith. King Solomon, according to the Bible, built the First Temple of the Jews on this mountaintop circa 1000 B.C., only to have it torn down 400 years later by troops commanded by the Babylonian king Nebuchadnezzar who sent many Jews into exile. In the first century, B.C. Herod expanded and refurbished a Second Temple built by Jews who had returned after their banishment. It is here, according to the Gospel of John, Jesus

Christ lashed out against the moneychangers (and was later crucified a few hundred yards away). The Roman general Titus exacted revenge against Jewish rebels, sacking and burning the Temple in A.D. 70." [1]

John 3

Nicodemus, a Pharisee and a member of the Jewish ruling council makes a secret visit to Jesus no doubt to avoid being seen by his peers. He may be part of the ruling class that feels threatened by Jesus' popularity but his first words reveal a recognition of and a reverence for the man, Jesus.

"Rabbi," he says, *"we know you are a teacher who has come from God. For no one could perform the signs you are doing if God were not with him."*

The exchange between the two men confronts us with a challenging matter. Listen carefully as Jesus answers Nicodemus. Jesus told Nicodemus that no one could see the Kingdom of God unless he is *"born again."*

The Greek word used here can mean either "again" or "from above." Nicodemus took the meaning to be "again" and asked *"how can someone be born when he is old?"* He was interpreting Jesus' meaning as being physical as in "entering again into his mother's womb". In other words, Nicodemus was not seeing things through spiritual eyes but only through natural eyes.

Jesus clarified with these words, *"Flesh gives birth to flesh, but the Spirit gives birth to spirit."*

---

[1] A territorial prize occupied or conquered by a long succession of peoples including Jebusites, Israelites, Babylonians, Greeks, Persians, Romans, Byzantines, early Muslims, Crusaders, Mamluks, Ottomans, and the British — the Temple Mount has seen more momentous historical events than perhaps any other 35 acres in the world." (Hammer, 2001).

Later scripture would clearly state that this new birth comes only by believing in Jesus as the Savior sent from God and by accepting Jesus as Lord and Savior, thus the meaning "from above" to which Christ referred.

Jesus added this. *"The Son of Man must be lifted up, that everyone who believes may have eternal life in him."*

[John 3:1–15]

> - **If you could ask Jesus some questions about what it means to be born again, what would you ask him?**
> - **What does being born again mean to you?**

The words that follow this exchange between Jesus and Nicodemus are, perhaps, the most often quoted words from the Bible.

Jesus explained, *"For God so loved the world that he gave his one and only Son, that whoever believes in him shall not perish but have eternal life. For God did not send his Son into the world to condemn the world, but to save the world through him."*

However, there was a problem. Jesus went on to say, *"Light has come into the world, but people loved darkness instead of light because their deeds were evil. Everyone who does evil hates the light, and will not come into the light for fear that their deeds will be exposed."*

[John 3:16–21]

- What does the passage that begins with the words "God so loved the world" mean?
- What is the meaning of the statement "men loved darkness instead of light"? Do you see any evidence of this in our own time?
- What is it about living in the light that makes it a worthwhile goal?

In this battle between light and darkness lies the destiny of every person's soul. Jesus reaches out to us through the darkness, bringing light with him. It is at this point that each person must make a choice to believe and be "born from above" or to remain in sin and darkness and to eventually be eternally cut off from God.

FOR FURTHER DISCUSSION OR PERSONAL REFLECTION:

[JOHN 2:13-25]

Why did Jesus forcefully remove moneychangers and sellers of sacrificial animals from the temple court?

If you were a public relations consultant to Jesus, would you have advised him to do this cleansing thing so early in his ministry? Why or why not?

[JOHN 3:16]

Why has John 3:16 become such a well-known scripture?

SESSION 4

WHY DID JESUS MEET WITH SOCIETY'S OUTCASTS?

John 4:1–5:47

There is an interesting phrase in chapter 4 which reads, "He (Jesus) had to go through Samaria . . ." Technically this was not true. The Jews avoided passing through Samaria, a region in the central part of nation that was principally occupied by a despised people who were not considered to be full-blooded Jews. Jewish travelers would go out of their way to avoid Samaria, even crossing the Jordan River and spending part of their journey in a foreign land.

However, Jesus "had to go through Samaria" because a certain Samaritan woman had an appointment with destiny. Even though she was not aware of the meeting, Jesus knew of their encounter at the well that would change her life and the lives of the people in her entire village.

As he passed through Samaria on his way from Judea to Galilee, Jesus paused for rest by a well called "Jacob's well." While his disciples had gone into town to purchase food, a Samaritan woman came to draw water from the well and was drawn into a deep conversation with Jesus. Jesus began the conversation by asking her for a drink of water. When Jesus spoke to the Samaritan woman she was surprised because she was very aware that Jews did not associate with Samaritans

[John 4:1–9]

> There was considerable racial and ethnic animosity between the Jews and the Samaritans. Can you identify any people today who are viewed as Samaritans were in Jesus' time?

This private conversation also violated certain mores of that period since it was considered improper for an unconnected man and woman to converse in such a manner, especially with no one else present. When the woman voiced her surprise, Jesus responded by telling her that, if she had known the one with whom she spoke, she would have requested and been given *living water*. He added that the water he offered would eliminate thirst and would well up to eternal life. She was interested in the offer of this miraculous water and said she would indeed like to receive this water. An instructive exchange followed.

When Jesus told her to go get her husband and return she spoke candidly and honestly by telling him that she had no husband. Jesus responded that she was right — she previously had five husbands and the man with whom she was currently living was not her husband.

[John 4:10-17]

> Why did this woman's past not have an impact on Jesus' determination to lead her to salvation?

Despite her past and the enmity between Jews and Samaritans, Jesus would not allow those reasons to exclude the woman and her village from the gift of salvation. This powerful statement still applies to us today.

He said, *"a time is coming and has now come when the true worshipers will worship the Father in spirit and truth, for they are the kinds of worshipers the Father seeks. God is spirit, and his worshipers must worship in spirit and in truth."*

The woman responded, *"I know that Messiah (called Christ) is coming. When he comes he will explain everything to us."*

Then Jesus declared, *"I who speak to you am he."*

It was at this point that the disciples returned. The woman left her water jars, returned to her town, and told those of her village, *"Come, see a man who told me everything I ever did. Could this be the Messiah?"*

Those she spoke with made their way to see Jesus, and believed in him in because of the testimony of this woman. They urged Jesus to stay with them and he stayed there for two days. While he was there, many more villagers became believers. They told the woman that they no longer believed just because of what she said but because of what they themselves had heard. *"We know that this man is the Savior of the world."*

[John 4:17–42]

- **The Bible tells us that the people from the woman's village stated that they no longer believed just because of what she had said but that they believed because they had heard Jesus for themselves. Why did Jesus personal interaction have such an effect on the villagers?**
- **What do you believe was going through the minds of the disciples while Jesus was bringing the gospel to the Samaritans?**

This surprising exchange between Jesus and the Samaritan woman is related in John's usual, somewhat dramatic fashion. At the same time, it seems to be no more significant than any of the other accounts given to us by John. However it contains revelations regarding God and his desired relationship with mankind that have made this fourth chapter of John required reading for every Christian.

- It demonstrates that Jesus does not recognize the ethnic, racial, and social barriers put into place by man. The fact that the woman was a Samaritan and that he was interacting with her in a setting that was frowned upon by the society of his day did not matter to Jesus. Two things mattered: she was a soul in need of salvation and he was that Savior.

- It reveals to us that Jesus knows everything about us. Jesus knew that the woman had what was, and still is, considered a checkered past and yet he engaged her in a conversation that led to her salvation.

- It reveals the true nature of God. God is spirit in essence. He is not "a" spirit, He is purely Spirit. He has no bodily form as we know it. There are times in the Bible when we see God pictured as having a body but these are only at times when God chooses to reveal himself in such a way in order to convey a message or relate to the person with whom he is interacting.

- It shows us the true nature of worship. Jesus said, *"God is spirit, and his worshipers must worship in spirit and in truth"*

[John 4:1–54]

- What did Jesus mean when he said that God's worshipers *"must worship in spirit and in truth"*?
- How can we participate in this a spiritual connection with God?
- How does our physical posture, religious position, social standing, geographical location or other distinctives affect our worship of God?

John 5

Jesus returned to Jerusalem for a Jewish feast. A pool near the Sheep Gate was thought to have healing qualities. On occasion, the waters would "stir" about and many believed that when the water in the pool was stirred, those who were able to get into the pool would be healed of their sickness. Some may have even believed that it was an angel who came and caused the water to move. Regardless of the source of the movement of the water, many who were blind, lame, or paralyzed gathered by the pool in hopes that they could get into the water when it was stirred so they could be healed.

One of them was a man who had been an invalid for 38 years. Jesus saw him and asked, *"Do you want to get well?"* to which the man responded that he had been unable to get in the pool at the right time. Jesus' response was quite direct.

"Get up! Pick up your mat and walk."

The man picked up his mat and walked, but again there was a problem. This event happened on the Sabbath, and the Jewish leaders told the man that the Law forbade him to carry his mat on the Sabbath. When the man told them what had happened to him, they asked the man by whom he had been healed. The man had no idea who it was because Jesus had slipped away into the crowd.

Later, Jesus found him at the temple and spoke to him and told him to stop sinning or something worse could happen to him. The man then told the Jewish leaders that Jesus was the one who had made him well.

[John 5:1–15]

> Why do you believe that Jesus either performed miracles secretively or quickly slipped away, hiding himself in the crowd following the performance of a miracle?

Because Jesus did this on the Sabbath, "the Jewish leaders began to persecute him." This led to what would be one of several defining moments in Jesus' earthly ministry. Jesus referred to "his Father" who was always at work as was he, Jesus, the Son. The Jewish leaders then accused him of not only breaking the Sabbath but of "calling God his own Father, making himself equal with God." The phrase "equal with God" conveyed independence from God. Jesus acknowledged more than an affinity with God; he claimed identity with God.

Jesus responded that he would show them even greater things. For example, he said, the Father had entrusted the Son with all judgment.

Jesus added: *"whoever hears my word and believes him who sent me has eternal life and will not be judged but has crossed over from death to life."*

Even the dead will hear the voice of the Son of God and those who hear will live. *"A time is coming when all who are in their graves will hear his voice and come out—those who have done good will rise to live, and those who have done evil will rise to be condemned."*

[John 5:16–47]

- **This is one of several times that Jesus' conflict with the Jewish leaders arose from the performance of miracles on the Sabbath. What does this tell us about Jesus attitude toward the law? What does it tell us about the true spiritual condition of the Jewish leaders?**
- **Why do you think that Jesus did not use his power to silence his critics rather than allowing them to continue even to the moment of his death?**

It was obvious that Jesus was choosing the time and manner in which he would reveal his identity as the Son of God. Most of those who received or witnessed a miracle, those who had the least to lose in this life, had little difficulty believing that Jesus was God's Son. Almost all of those who had riches, power and influence in this life would reject Jesus' statements and only see their hearts grow harder against him.

FOR FURTHER DISCUSSION OR PERSONAL REFLECTION:

[JOHN 4:1-42]
What is the Living Water of which Jesus spoke?

[JOHN 5:1-15]
When Jesus spoke to the man by the pool at the Sheep Gate, he could see that the man was obviously lame. Why did he ask the man if he wanted to be made well?

[JOHN 5:16-47]
What do you think about Jesus' statement that *"even the dead will hear the voice of the Son of God and those who hear will live"*?

Do you see yourself living in eternal life? If so, how?

SESSION 5

WHY IS IT HARD TO UNDERSTAND SOME OF JESUS' TEACHINGS?

John 6:1–7:52

The miraculous signs that Jesus performed attracted crowds to him and although many did not understand the depth of his teachings, Jesus had compassion on them. On one occasion when it was mealtime, Jesus used a boy's five small barley loaves and two small fish to feed a crowd of 5,000 men and their families. When the people saw this they proclaimed that Jesus was "The Prophet" who was to come, basically calling him the Messiah. But Jesus withdrew to a mountain alone.

There could be several reasons that Jesus withdrew from the people. One of the most significant reasons is that they were not seeking Jesus with the proper motives in their hearts. By this point in Jesus' ministry, he was quite famous for the miracles that he performed. These miracles attracted crowds wherever he went and sometimes attracted crowds so large that they could be difficult to manage. In this instance, John states that "Jesus, knowing that they intended to come and make him king by force, withdrew again to a mountain by himself." This would not be the last time that Jesus would be forced to deal with people who sought him for the wrong reasons.

[John 6:1–15]

- Why would the crowds who followed Jesus assume that, because he could multiply fish and bread, he should be king?
- It seems that Jesus often went up into the mountains. What do you believe he was doing during these times and why?

That evening, Jesus' disciples set out in a boat to cross the lake bound for Capernaum. The disciples were finding it difficult to row across the lake due to a strong opposing wind. As the disciples labored with their rowing, Jesus came to them walking on the water. When the disciples saw Jesus, they were terrified because, as another gospel account states, "they thought he was a ghost" (Matthew 14:26) Jesus soothed their fears by telling them, *"It is I, don't be afraid."* Jesus got into the boat and they proceeded to the other side of the lake.

The next morning the crowd discovered that Jesus was gone. Word reached them that Jesus had gone to the other side of the lake during the night. So, the crowds pursued Jesus. When the crowds reached him, they asked him when he had arrived in Capernaum. It is here that Jesus began to speak to them very plainly regarding their motives while also speaking to them in spiritual terms regarding what should be their proper motives. It is also here that many, not understanding the spiritual concepts of which Jesus spoke, stopped following Jesus.

[John 6:16–24]

> **Why do you believe it is difficult for those who do not have a spiritual relationship with Christ to understand some of his teachings?**

Jesus noted that they were seeking him because of the miraculous sign of the multiplication of the bread and fish and because they had eaten their fill. Jesus went on to say that they should instead seek nourishment that does not spoil, food that brings eternal life. Then they asked: *"What must we do to do the works God requires?"*

His response was, *"The work of God is this: to believe in the one he has sent."*

The people then asked for another miraculous sign to which Jesus responded, *"I am the bread of life. He who comes to me will never go hungry, and he who believes in me will never be thirsty . . . For my Father's will is that everyone who looks to the Son and believes in him shall have eternal life, and I will raise him up at the last day."*

The Jews could hardly believe what they were hearing. *"Is this not Jesus, the son of Joseph, whose father and mother we know?"* They wondered how he could make these claims. Jesus had tried to connect with them through their own history, but they could not fathom his teaching. These exchanges took place in the synagogue in Capernaum.

[John 6:17–44]

> - How should we understand Jesus calling himself the bread of life?
> - What does Jesus mean when he says, *"I will raise him up at the last day."*

What follows is a real challenge to understand. Jesus spoke of eating the flesh of the Son of Man and drinking his blood.

He says, *"my flesh is real food and my blood is real drink. Whoever eats my flesh and drinks my blood remains in me, and I in him."*

It was this teaching of Christ's body being "the bread of life" coupled with his reference to the drinking of his blood being the only way to eternal life that caused many in the crowd to say, *"This is a hard teaching. Who can accept it?"*

There are few things more repugnant to a Jew than the thought of eating human flesh or drinking any kind of blood. Since their hearts were not prepared to understand that Jesus was speaking of spiritual concepts and not physical, they completely misunderstood what Jesus was saying and they stopped following him. In Matthew's gospel account, Jesus said: *"He who has ears, let him hear"* (Matthew 11:18). This admonition is the key to understanding what Jesus is saying about his flesh and blood, as well as other passages of scripture that sometimes baffle us.

The assumption here was not that many in the crowds had no ears, rather Jesus was referring to those who were able to "hear" or "understand" the spiritual nature of what he was saying. Jesus said, *"The words that I have spoken to you are spirit and they are life. Yet there are some of you who do not believe."*

[John 6:45–64]

> ■ **What does Jesus want us to hear and understand?**

There will be times during our Christian lives when we will not understand what God is saying in his word or doing in our lives. It is in those times that we must pray for faith, patience and understanding and refuse to stop following God simply because we cannot interpret everything that he says in his Word or understand everything that is happening in our lives.

When Jesus challenged the Twelve, *"You do not want to leave me too, do you?"*

Peter responded, *"Lord, to whom shall we go? You have the words of eternal life. We have come to believe and to know that you are the Holy One of God."*

At this, Jesus announced that one of the Twelve would betray him. He meant Judas, the son of Simon Iscariot.

[John 6:65–71]

> ■ **Have you ever been baffled with the teachings of Jesus? What brought clarification for you?**

John 7

Jesus stayed in Galilee because the Jewish leaders in Judea were trying to entrap him. His brothers urged him to go public with his claims during the Feast of Tabernacles in Judea to which Jesus replied that he would show up when the time was right. John tells us, however, that even his brothers did not really believe in him. After his brothers left for the Feast, Jesus went also, but in secret. Jerusalem was abuzz with whispers about Jesus. Many said he was a good man, but they were afraid to speak their views in public because they feared the Jewish leaders. Others who believed that Jesus deceived the people did not need to be so discreet in expressing their opinions.

> **Why do you believe that Jesus' brothers did not believe that he was the Messiah?**

Halfway through the Feast, Jesus went to the Temple courts and began to teach. The Jews were amazed by his learning because he had not had the benefit of formal education. In his exchanges, Jesus noted that Moses gave his people the Law, but no one was keeping that Law, that they observed the Sabbath according to the Law but thought it inappropriate for Jesus to heal on the Sabbath.

"Stop judging by mere appearances," said Jesus.

There was chatter in the crowd about where Jesus was from since it was thought that Christ would come from Bethlehem. In spite of all this, many did believe in Jesus. The chief priests and Pharisees sent temple guards to arrest Jesus.

[John 7:1–29]

- Since Jesus had no formal education, how did he possess such a great understanding of scripture?
- What do you think Jesus meant by, "Stop judging by mere appearances"? Is this something that applies to us today?

On the last day of the Feast, Jesus stood up and proclaimed, *"Whoever believes in me, as the Scripture has said, streams of living water will flow from within him."*

Here he is talking about the Holy Spirit who will follow Jesus and indwell those who believed in Jesus. Finally, the temple guards went back to the chief priests and Pharisees, who asked them, *"Why didn't you bring him in?"* The guards replied: *"No one ever spoke the way this man does."*

Nicodemus, a ruler of the synagogue with whom Jesus had spoken earlier about being born again, asked, *"Does our law condemn a man without first hearing him to find out what he has been doing?"* Their response sidestepped the question. *"You will find,"* they answered, *"that a prophet does not come out of Galilee."*

[John 7:30–52]

- Why do the Pharisees ignore both the temple guards who were sent to arrest Jesus and one of their own who raises a point of law?

FOR FURTHER DISCUSSION OR PERSONAL REFLECTION:

[JOHN 6:1-15]
What is your understanding of the feeding of the 5,000?

[JOHN 7:36-38]
We are told that the *"streams of living water"* that would flow within those who believed in Jesus was the Spirit that those who believed in him would receive later. What do you associate with the metaphor *"streams of living water"*?

[JOHN 6,7]
If you could ask Jesus additional questions at this point, what would they be?

SESSION 6

WHAT DOES IT MEAN TO BE A SLAVE OF SIN?
John 8

Most sinners would tell Christians that we are the ones who are in bondage. Sinners believe that believers are restricted by what they see as the rules and regulations of our faith. This misunderstanding of the freedom brought about by placing our faith in Christ as our savior demonstrates the blinding effects of sin. Those who engage in a life of sin are slaves to the things that they think they enjoy. This subtle lie of Satan will cause many to reject Christ, the only source of true freedom.

It was dawn in the temple courts and crowds had gathered around Jesus. As he taught, the teachers of the Law and Pharisees brought to him a woman caught in adultery. They stood the woman before the crowd and reminded Jesus that the Law of Moses required that such women be stoned. (According to Old Testament law, only engaged virgins were subject to this punishment.) *"Now what do you say?"* the accusers asked Jesus.

They were setting a trap to justify a legal case against him. If he said that the woman should be forgiven he would be accused of not abiding by the law and condoning immorality. If he said she should be stoned he would be accused of having no compassion. And, if he argued for the woman because she had technically not committed a sin worthy of stoning, he would be accused of condoning immorality and allowing the woman a free pass on a technicality.

One person conspicuously missing from this scene is the man with whom the woman was committing adultery. According to Old Testament law, many forms of adultery called for both parties to be stoned rather than stoning the woman only.

Christ's reaction to their obvious trap was interesting. As they continued questioning him, Jesus stooped down and wrote on the ground with his finger. Then he stood up and said, *"If any of you is without sin, let him be the first to throw a stone at her."*

Jesus then stooped down and again began to write on the ground with his finger. The accusers began to walk away, beginning with the oldest and ending with the youngest, until only Jesus was left with the woman. *"Has no one condemned you?"* he asked.

"No one, sir," she said.

"Then neither do I condemn you," Jesus declared. *"Go now and leave your life of sin."*

[John 8:1–11]

- Is judging others appropriate only for those who have not sinned? Why or why not?
- Was the charge against the woman valid? Why or why not?

Jesus continued the verbal sparring with the Pharisees over what constituted valid testimony and about his relationship with God the Father. He angered the Pharisees when he proclaimed: *"I am the light of the world, whoever follows me will never walk in darkness but will have the light of life."* They wanted to know who, besides himself, could validate that claim.

Jesus did not mince words when he responded, *"When you have lifted up the Son of Man, then you will know that I am he and that I do nothing on my own but speak just what the Father has taught me. The one who sent me is with me; he has not left me alone, for I always do what pleases him."* John reports that as Jesus spoke many put their faith in him.

It is interesting to note that, during this exchange, of those who believed in Jesus no Pharisees, Sadducees, priests, or teachers are mentioned as being among the believers. So often, those who think themselves to be wise are among the most ignorant of all people. Those who were humble enough to know that they needed the Messiah, placed their faith in Jesus with gladness. Pride does, indeed, proceed a person's downfall.

[John 8:12–30]

- What did Jesus mean when he said, *"when you have lifted up the Son of Man"*?
- There is no evidence that most of Jesus' accusers came to know him to be the One he claimed to be. How do you explain his prediction that they would know this?

Jesus continued to teach by saying this to the Jews who believed him: *"If you hold to my teaching, you are really my disciples. Then you will know the truth, and the truth will set you free."*

They responded by saying that, as Abraham's descendants, they had never been slaves of anyone. Apparently, they were forgetting over 430 years of bondage in Egypt, the many times they were enslaved by various Canaanite tribes in the time of the Judges, and the Babylonian captivity. They were also ignoring the steady progression of Gentile kingdoms that had held Israel under their heels culminating in the Roman army who occupied the land in Jesus' day and who would eventually destroy Jerusalem, razing it to the ground. Their denial only emphasizes the truth of Jesus' next words, words that every Christian should remember and every sinner should hear.

"Everyone who sins is a slave to sin." In this statement, he shows us the humiliation and progressive degradation brought about by a life of sin.

[John 8:31–36]

- What did Jesus mean when he said that the truth will set us free? (John 8:32)
- What did Jesus mean when he said, "If anyone keeps my word, he will never see death?" (John 8:51)

As Jesus continued, he made the following statements about himself:

"If God were your Father, you would love me, for I came from God."

- "Because I tell the truth, you do not believe me! . . . If I am telling the truth, why don't you believe me?"
- "Can any of you prove me guilty of sin?"
- "Whoever belongs to God hears what God says."
- "You do not hear because you do not belong to God."
- "I am not possessed by a demon, [as the Jewish leaders purported] but I honor my Father and you dishonor me."
- "Whoever obeys my word, he will never see death."

[John 8:37–51]

> What word of Jesus must one obey to enjoy eternal life?

John 9

As Jesus and his disciples continued through the city, they encountered a man born blind. The disciples asked Jesus whether the blindness was from the man's sins or his parents' sins. During that time, most Jews were taught that a person's state in life was due to sin, either sins committed by the afflicted person's parents or by the person himself. This false teaching was passed down throughout the centuries by the rabbis and teachers of the law through a distorted interpretation of Moses' writings. It applied not only to a person's physical maladies but even to their financial and social standing in the Jewish culture. If a person was healthy, wealthy, or well respected by his peers he was assumed to be pleasing to God.

Jesus responded to His disciples by saying that the man's blindness was neither from his or his parents' sins but was there so that the work of God might be displayed in this life. Jesus healed the man's blindness in a most unusual way. He spit into some clay on the ground and mixed it into a sort of paste. He then applied the sticky paste to the man's eyes and told him to go and wash his face in the pool of Siloam.

[John 9:1-6]

> - **Why do people often attribute people's tough circumstances to sin?**
> - **What does Jesus response to his disciples' questions about responsibility for sin tell us about God?**

The scriptures do not record that the blind man asked to be healed. Neither do we have a record that the man asked who Jesus was or why he had put mud on his face. In fact, we know that he did not ask who Jesus was because, when asked who had healed him, he told them that he didn't know. It is quite amazing that this blind man would obey the words of a stranger who had just rubbed mud on his vacant eyes but then it is amazing what people will do when they are desperate.

Most of the poor blind people ended up as beggars. He was probably sitting by the road and begging for coins from those who passed by. As to why he obeyed Jesus, we can only speculate. Perhaps he thought that, if he did as the stranger said, he would receive several coins for his trouble. Perhaps it was the forcefulness of Christ's presence. What we do know is that the man was blind but was healed and fully regained his eyesight. Those who had known the blind man were amazed and asked about the man who healed him.

Friends and acquaintances brought the man to the Pharisees. However, the Pharisees, still slaves to the letter of the law and not knowing the spirit in which the law was given, said that Jesus could not be from God because he did this on the Sabbath. The religious leaders had the man's parents brought to them and asked if their son had, in fact, been born blind. If so, how was it that he could now see?

"He was born blind," answered the parents, *"but how he can see now, or who opened his eyes, we don't know."*

They proposed that the leaders ask their son to speak for himself. Even if his parents knew who had healed their son they might have been reluctant to say so because the religious leaders had decided that anyone who acknowledged that Jesus was the Christ would be put out of the synagogue.

[John 9:7–23]

- **According to historians, Pharisees of Jesus' day had refined the act of clothing themselves in their robes to the point that their entire garment could be held in place with only one small pin. This way, they would bear no more burden than was necessary on the Sabbath and thus, not be in danger of breaking the laws of doing no work on the Sabbath.**

- **Why do you believe that the Pharisees were such fanatics about every tiny point of the law?**

The religious leaders again summoned the man born blind and tried to get him to say that Jesus was a sinner. His reply was classic. *"Whether he is a sinner or not, I don't know. One thing I do know, I was blind but now I see."*

After a few more exchanges, the man said with courage, *"We know that God does not listen to sinners. He listens to the godly man who does his will. Nobody has ever heard of opening the eyes of a man born blind. If this man were not from God, he could do nothing."*

"How dare you lecture us!" replied the leaders, and they threw him out.

When Jesus heard about this, he found the man and asked him, *"Do you believe in the Son of Man?"* The man asked who the Son of Man might be so that he might believe in him.

Jesus responded, *"You have now seen him; in fact, he is the one speaking with you."*

Then the man said, *"Lord, I believe,"* and he worshipped Jesus.

[John 9:24–38]

- Are you able to make a statement similar to that made by the man born blind when he said, *"One thing I know, I was blind and now can see"*? (John 9:25)

- Jesus healing of the man born blind opened his eyes physically and spiritually. What is it about Jesus that shapes your own relationship to him?

This story is typical of believers and sinners in that day and today. Those who know they are blind, whether their blindness is physical or spiritual, recognize their condition and open themselves to the help that only Christ can offer. On the other hand, the self-righteous seldom allow their views to be debated or questioned. Because of this, they remain blind and in bondage to their sins.

FOR FURTHER DISCUSSION OR PERSONAL REFLECTION:

[JOHN 8:1-11]

Does it surprise you that the incident with the woman caught in adultery occurred at dawn in the temple courts with crowds already present? Why or why not?

What was Jesus' aim in pointing out that judging others was appropriate only for those who have not sinned?

In light of Jesus' telling the woman that she should leave her life of sin, what do you think this woman told her friends about this experience?

[JOHN 9: 1-41]

I what ways are you spiritually blind? How does that affect your relationship with God and your relationships with others?

What will it take to restore your spiritual vision?

SESSION 7

WHY DOES JESUS IDENTIFY AS A SHEPHERD?

John 10:1–11:57

Jesus spent a lot of time trying to disclose his identity to help those who heard and saw him to believe in him. His references to sheep and a shepherd would not only have resonated with those engaged in farming, but also with those who studied scripture and associated sheep with sacrifice and with David, the one-time shepherd boy and their most revered king.

"*Very truly I tell you Pharisees,*" Jesus begins, "*anyone who does not enter the sheep pen by the gate, but climbs in by some other way, is a thief and a robber. The one who enters by the gate is the shepherd of the sheep. The gatekeeper opens the gate for him, and the sheep listen to his voice. He calls his own sheep by name and leads them out. When he has brought out all his own, he goes on ahead of them, and his sheep follow him because they know his voice. But they will never follow a stranger; in fact, they will run away from him because they do not recognize a stranger's voice.*" Jesus used this figure of speech, but the Pharisees did not understand what he was telling them.

"***I am the gate** for the sheep,*" said Jesus. "*Those who enter through me will be saved . . . I have come that they may have life and have it to the full.*"

"***I am the good shepherd.** The good shepherd lays down his life for the sheep.*"

"***I know my sheep and my sheep know me** — just as the Father knows me and I know the Father — and I lay down my life for the sheep.*"

"***I have other sheep that are not of this sheep pen.** I must bring them also. They too will listen to my voice, and there shall be one flock and one shepherd.*"

[John 10:1–16]

> **Why would Jesus use so many analogies regarding sheep and shepherds to explain his relationship with those who believe in him as Messiah?**

Hearers were divided in their response to Jesus. The Jewish leaders asked him to tell them plainly if he was the Christ. He responded that the miracles he did in his Father's name spoke for him.

"*You do not believe,*" he added, "*because you are not my sheep.*"

Some who heard him picked up stones to stone him.

"*For which of the miracles do you stone me?*" asked Jesus.

They replied that their stoning was for his blasphemy — because he, a mere man, was claiming to be God.

[John 10:17–33]

> **In what way is Jesus claiming to be God in his references to sheep and shepherds?**

John spent time telling us about Lazarus and his sisters, Mary and Martha. A special note is made that this Mary was the one who "anointed" Jesus with perfume and wiped his feet with her hair. John specifically mentioned that Jesus loved Lazarus and that he loved Martha and Mary as well. Since the Jewish leaders were seeking a reason to have Jesus put to death he had been ministering in areas away from Jerusalem because he knew that the time of his sacrifice was close but that it had not yet arrived. However, the sisters, knowing that this was a matter of life for death for their brother, sent word to Jesus regarding Lazarus' serious condition.

When word arrived of his friend's sickness, Jesus told his disciples that Lazarus was asleep and that they needed to go wake him up. The disciples, misunderstanding Jesus' meaning, said that, if Lazarus was sick it would be good for him to find rest in sleep. At this point, Jesus says plainly to his disciples, *"Lazarus is dead... But let us go to him."*

When they neared Bethany they found that Lazarus was dead and had been in the tomb for four days. Martha met them and said to Jesus, *"If you had been here, my brother would not have died."*

Jesus responded, *"Your brother will rise again."*

Martha acknowledged that her brother would rise in the resurrection at the last day, but Jesus said to her, *"I am the* resurrection and the life. He who believes in me will live, even though he dies, and whoever lives and believes in me will never die."

Then he confronted Martha with the question, *"Do you believe this?"* She answered not only with a *"yes"* but confessed her belief that Jesus was the Christ, the Son of God.

Martha went to let Mary know that Jesus was almost there. Mary and those who had gathered to mourn with the family went to meet Jesus. She expressed the same faith as her sister that if Jesus had been there her brother would be alive. When Jesus asked where they had laid Lazarus they replied, *"Come and see."* When Jesus saw the sorrow of his friends he was deeply moved. After this, we have the shortest verse in the Bible: *"Jesus wept."*

[John 11:1–37]

> ■ **Since Jesus knew that he was about to raise Lazarus from the dead, why do you think that he wept at the tomb?**

When they reached the cave where they had placed Lazarus' body, Jesus commanded that the entry stone be taken away. At this command, Martha protested saying that, since Lazarus' body had been placed in the tomb four days before Jesus' arrival, the body would have the strong and unpleasant odor of decomposition. Jesus answered her with a question.

"Did I not tell you that, if you believed, you would see the glory of God?"

For the benefit of those gathered there, Jesus offered a prayer that they might believe that God had sent him.

A fact that is seldom discussed is that, although the Jews were God's people and believed in him as the One true God, they still held to some rabbinical superstitions that had been passed down through the years and were found in somewhat obscure passages in the Mishnah, (revered rabbinical writings not included in sacred scripture). One of those superstitions was that, when a person died, their spirit stayed close to the body for three days prior to going into the presence of their father, Abraham. The spirit would seek an opportunity to reenter the body if possible but if, after three days, it had not been able to reenter the body, it would pass into the "bosom of Abraham". This is a possible explanation of why Jesus chose to wait until the body had been interred for four days. He wanted there to be no doubt as to the Glory of God that was to be revealed by this resurrection.

The Bible tells us that Jesus called in a loud voice, *"Lazarus, come out!"* The dead man came out, his hands and feet wrapped with strips of linen, and a cloth around his face. Then Jesus said to the stunned onlookers, *"Take off the grave clothes and let him go."*

With this and what had gone before, many believed in Jesus and his claim to be the Christ, the Messiah.

[John 11:38–45]

> ■ When Jesus answers Martha, *"... if you believed, you would see the glory of God?"* what is he suggesting about her level of skepticism? How does that statement apply to you?

As difficult as it might be to imagine – there were still some who did not believe. After this event, the chief priests and Pharisees called a meeting of the Sanhedrin to consider their options. *"If we let him go on like this,"* they said, *"everyone will believe in him and the Romans will come and take over our nation."* Rome, they knew, could not tolerate someone with this kind of power amassing a constituency that would pose a threat to Roman rule. Caiaphas, the high priest for that year, spoke up and warned that it was better for one man to die than for the whole nation to perish. So, from that day, they plotted to take Jesus' life.

[John 11:46–57]

FOR FURTHER DISCUSSION OR PERSONAL REFLECTION:

[JOHN 10:9]
What did Jesus mean when he said, *"I am the gate for the sheep"*?

[JOHN 10:1-11:57]
What questions would you like to ask Jesus about the statements he made in this segment?

SESSION 8

WHAT DOES JESUS WANT HIS FOLLOWERS TO UNDERSTAND?

John 12

With his impending trial and crucifixion, Jesus knew that he had to prepare his disciples for the time when he would no longer be with them. Despite all of his teaching and working of miracles, Jesus knew that his followers were not prepared for what lay ahead.

Jesus and his disciples withdrew to the village of Ephraim. It was almost time for the Jewish Passover Feast and people were expecting Jesus to attend this important holy day celebrating Israel's deliverance from slavery in Egypt. As usual, they expected Jesus eventually to make his way to the temple. Six days before the Passover, Jesus went back to Bethany to the home of Lazarus and his sisters, Mary and Martha. There, a dinner was given in Jesus honor. Martha served dinner while Lazarus and the other men in attendance reclined around the table.

It was during this time that Mary brought about a pint of pure nard, an expensive perfume, and poured it on Jesus' feet and began to wipe his feet with her hair. John specifically records that the house was filled with the fragrance of the perfume. The Bible tells us that the perfume was worth a year's wages and that Judas

Iscariot, the one who would betray Jesus, was the only person who objected to this act of sacrifice and worship. Judas asked, *"Why wasn't this perfume sold and the money given to the poor? It was worth a year's wages."*

John tells us that Judas' objection was not motivated by a sense of Christian love or altruism. Rather, Judas did this because he was the treasurer for the disciples, and, being a thief, he regularly helped himself to what was put in the common purse. Jesus defended the act as preparation for his burial and added, *"You will always have the poor among you, but you will not always have me."*

[John 12:1–8]

> - **Mary's pouring out, or anointing, of Jesus feet with the expensive oil was referred to by Jesus as *"for the day of his burial"*. (John 12:7) What do you think that Jesus meant by this?**
> - **Might Judas have been justified in questioning extravagance at the expense of the poor? How does the church decide how to allocate resources? Do the needy ever get shortchanged?**

As this scene was playing out inside Lazarus' home, a large crowd began to gather outside. Some came to see Jesus but many came to see Lazarus because they had heard that Jesus had raised him from the dead. Because they were aware of Lazarus' death and subsequent resurrection, many Jews had come to believe in Jesus. When word of this reached the chief priests, they made plans to kill Lazarus as well as Jesus.

John writes that, "The next day the crowd that had come for the Feast heard that Jesus was on his way into Jerusalem. They took palm branches and went out to meet him shouting, 'Hosanna! Blessed is he who comes in the name of the Lord!'"

Jesus set out for Jerusalem to complete the ultimate act of sacrifice on behalf of humankind. At Christ's direction, the disciples had secured a young donkey on which he rode into Jerusalem. This fulfilled that which was written by the prophet Zechariah when he said, *"Do not be afraid, O Daughter of Zion; see, your king is coming, seated on a donkey's colt."*

While the significance of Jesus arriving on a donkey may have not been recognized by many of the people, it certainly did not go unnoticed by the priests and Pharisees. They were aware that, according to Middle Eastern tradition, a king of war enters his city on a warhorse while a king who brings peace enters on a donkey, demonstrating that, in his humility, he brought peace. They were aware that either way, Jesus was declaring himself to be a king. The numbers of those who believed in Jesus as the Christ were on the increase as was the apprehension of the Pharisees and priests who said to one another, *"See, this is getting us nowhere. Look how the whole world has gone after him!"*

[John 12:9–19]

> ▪ **How does the recognition of Jesus coming as a King threaten the Pharisees and priests? How does his kingship threaten you?**

Some Greeks came to the Feast and sought out Philip to help them see Jesus. When Jesus heard about this he was prompted to say, *"The hour has come for the Son of Man to be glorified."* Jesus compared his anticipated death to a kernel of wheat that will remain a single seed unless it dies and is planted in the ground. Only then can it produce many seeds.

Jesus acknowledged that his heart was troubled and he asked, *". . . what shall I say? 'Father, save me from this hour'?"* He answered his own question by saying *"No, it was for this very reason that he had come to this hour."* Then Jesus prayed, *"Father, glorify your name!"*

A voice like thunder came from heaven saying, *"I have glorified it and will glorify it again."*

Jesus then declared that the prince of the world would be driven out by his action and that when he, Jesus, was lifted up from the earth, he would draw all men to himself. The words, *"lifted up from the earth"* indicated what kind of death he would suffer.

"Put your trust in the light while you have it," Jesus affirmed, *"so that you may become sons of light"*

"I have come into the world as a light," Jesus added, *"so that no one that believes in me should stay in darkness."*

[John 12:20–46]

> ■ On several occasions, the Bible mentions that Jesus would not allow certain things to happen because "his time had not yet come". When the Greeks came to Phillip, wishing to see Jesus, Christ said, *"The hour has come for the Son of Man to be glorified"* (John 12:23). What do you think made Jesus decide that his time had now come?

John tells us that, just as the prophets had foreseen many did not believe the Lord's message. Yet, at the same time, many did believe, even some of those among the Jewish leaders, though, they would not openly admit their belief because they feared the Pharisees.

Jesus affirmed that those who believed in him also believed in the one who had sent him. As for those who heard Jesus' words but did not keep them, he said he would not judge them. *"For I did not come to judge the world, but to save it."*

There would be a judge, however, for those who rejected Jesus and did not accept his words. They would be judged by Christ's words and their own rejection of the words that Jesus had spoken.

[John 12:47–50]

FOR FURTHER DISCUSSION OR PERSONAL REFLECTION:

[JOHN 12:24]
What is the significance of Jesus' comparison of what was about to happen to him with the kernel of wheat?

[JOHN 12:27]
John tells us that the heart of Jesus was troubled and he wondered about being saved from that hour. How do you explain the tension between Jesus the man and Jesus the Son of God?

SESSION 9

WHAT DOES JESUS MEAN WHEN HE SAYS "I HAVE OVERCOME THE WORLD"?

John 13:1-16:33

The next four chapters of the gospel of John are some of the most important of all scripture. Promises are made, events are explained, failures are prophesied and the seeds of betrayal, which had been sown for months, would come to full fruition. With the betrayal of Jesus just hours away, Christ pours himself into his disciples as fully and as rapidly as possible. Though this narrative covers but a few hours in the life of Jesus, entire books have been written to address each of the points covered in these four chapters. We will focus on the most vital of the spiritual concepts found in this discourse.

In those last hours, Jesus sought to strengthen his disciples. This was to prove to be a difficult exercise. At an evening meal just before the Passover Feast, Jesus got up, put a towel around his waist, poured water into a basin, and began to wash the feet of his disciples. This was an act ordinarily performed by servants or slaves, yet Jesus, God Incarnate, humbled himself to the role of a servant in order to demonstrate to his closest friends that the true nature of the Kingdom of God was found in serving and not in being served.

When he completed his task, Jesus interpreted what he had done, saying that his disciples should do the same for each other to demonstrate servant leadership.

"Very truly I tell you, no servant is greater than his master, nor is a messenger greater than the one who sent him." Jesus added, "Now that you know these things, you will be blessed if you do them."

[John 13:1–17]

- Could you humble yourself as Jesus did and wash another person's feet?
- How do Jesus' words serve as a warning to Christians to must beware of being influenced by a world system that promotes elevating one's self over others.
- How should Christians demonstrate this concept to a sinful world in order to personify the love and humility shown by Christ?

Jesus once again acknowledged that one of the Twelve would betray him. The disciples wanted to know who the culprit was. Jesus provided a clue that it would be Judas Iscariot. John reports that as Judas received from Jesus a piece of bread dipped in herbs, it was at that point Satan entered Judas. The betrayer quickly got up and left the room. He was going to see the chief priests in order to receive payment for his betrayal of Jesus.

[John 13:18–30]

> - What do you think was Judas' motivations in betraying Christ?
> - What do you believe the Bible means when it says of Judas that "Satan entered into him"?

While Jesus was trying to prepare his disciples for the shocking way in which he was to be beaten, mocked and killed during the following 12 hours, he offered a counterintuitive instruction. He didn't want his followers to let their sinful hearts guide their response to his death.

"A new command I give you:" he told them, *"Love one another. As I have loved you, so you must love one another. By this all men will know that you are my disciples if you love one another."*

As Jesus made reference to his departure, Simon Peter asked him where he was going. Jesus responded that he was going somewhere they could not go until later. Peter responded boldly, *"Why can't I follow you now? I will lay down my life for you."*

Jesus' response must have stirred up quite a concern among the disciples. *"Will you really do that?"* he asked Peter. *"Before the rooster crows, you will disown me three times."*

[John 13:31:38]

> - Peter promised that he would rather die than forsake Jesus even though later we find that he denied that he even knew Jesus. Have you ever failed a friend in such a way? Were you able to mend the relationship?

Jesus offered his disciples the assurance that he was going to his Father's house to prepare a place for them and that he would come back and take them with him so that they could be with him. Thomas spoke up and shared their uncertainty about where Jesus was going and asked, *"How can we know the way?"*

Jesus responded with a statement that is a cornerstone of Christianity when he said, *"I am the way and the truth and the life. No one comes to the Father except through me."*

This statement separates Christianity from all other religions. If Jesus is the only way, how can there be "many paths, one destination" as non-Christians have been saying for millennia.

Philip then asked that they be shown the Father, thinking that this revelation would cement their faith in him.

"Anyone who has seen me has seen the Father," Jesus told him and added, *"whoever believes in me will do the works I have been doing . . . You may ask me for anything in my name, and I will do it."*

[John 14:1:14]

- **Jesus affirmed that he was the way, the truth, and the life. What does this mean?**
- **What do you believe Jesus meant when he said, *"When you have seen me you have seen the Father"*?**

John seeks to unpack some of the mystery of these last words to the disciples with this new revelation from Jesus.

"If you love me, you will obey what I command. And I will ask the Father, and he will give you another Counselor to be with you forever — the Spirit of truth."

And there is more. *"I will not leave you as orphans; I will come to you. Before long, the world will not see me anymore, but you will see me. Because I live, you also will live."* Christians still hold to this promise today.

Jesus concluded the evening in the upper room with his disciples with these words: *"All this I have spoken while still with you. But the Counselor, the Holy Spirit, whom the Father will send in my name, will teach you all things and will remind you of everything I have said to you. Peace I leave with you; my peace I give you. I do not give to you as the world gives. Do not let your hearts be troubled and do not be afraid."*

Shortly after speaking these reassuring words, Jesus said, *"Come now, let us leave."*

After what seemed like parting words, John included important lessons that Jesus had been teaching to his disciples.

- Jesus said he was like a vine with branches. Branches that bear no fruit must be pruned to allow the fruit-bearing branches to produce more fruit. But these fruit-bearing branches must remain as part of the vine. The disciples cannot bear fruit unless they remain in Jesus. They are to bear much fruit to the glory of God.

[John 14:15–15:8]

- **What did Jesus mean by the analogy that he was the vine and the disciples were its branches?**
- **Why might the world hate Jesus' disciples and persecute them?**

- Jesus added to what he had said about love. *"Greater love has no one than this, that he lay down his life for his friends. You are my friends if you do what I command."*

- Jesus warned that the world would hate his disciples as it hated him first. They may be persecuted as he was persecuted. Those who hate him also hate the Father. But this, added Jesus, was to fulfill what was written in their Law about hating Christ without reason.

- Jesus gave them these instructions so that they would not go astray. They should expect to be put out of their synagogues. (As you can read elsewhere, the disciples would be killed by those who rejected the message of Jesus' free gift of spiritual salvation. Some of these killers believed that by killing Christ they were actually performing a service to God.).

- When the Counselor comes, Jesus said, *"he will prove the world to be in the wrong about sin and righteousness and judgment."*

- Understanding the anxiety his disciples felt about the future, Jesus offered this parallel: *"A woman giving birth to a child has pain because her time has come; but when her baby is born she forgets the anguish because of her joy that a child is born into the world. So with you."*

John reports that these last words made things clearer for the disciples because Jesus was speaking clearly without using figures of speech. They recognized Jesus' wisdom, and this helped them to believe that he came from God. Jesus ended this teaching with these words: *"In this world, you will have trouble. But take heart! I have overcome the world."*

[John 15:9–16:33]

FOR FURTHER DISCUSSION OR PERSONAL REFLECTION:

[JOHN 13:1-17]
What does servant leadership, as Jesus modeled it in washing his disciples' feet, mean to you?

[JOHN 14:6]
Jesus said no one comes to the Father except through him. What does this mean, and what implications does it have for those who say that "all religions are basically the same"?

[JOHN 14:15-31]
How will the Counselor who is to come convict the world of guilt in regard to sin?

[JOHN 13:1-16:33]
How did these last words of Jesus make things clearer for the disciples? Have they made things clearer for you? If so, how?

SESSION 10

HOW DID JESUS SPEND HIS LAST HOURS WITH THE DISCIPLES?

John 17:1–18:40

Following what must have been an evening that was taxing both physically and spiritually, Jesus and His disciples left the upper room bound for the Garden of Gethsemane. But before they left, Jesus offered a great prayer to God. This is the longest prayer by Jesus recorded in the Bible. He prayed for himself, for His disciples and for future believers who would come to salvation through the testimony of the disciples.

> It is at the beginning of this prayer that Jesus gives us an indication of the true nature of eternal life. As Jesus prayed, he said, *"Father, the time has come. Glorify your Son, that your Son may glorify you. For you granted him the authority over all people that he might give eternal life to all those you have given him. Now, this is eternal life: that they may know you, the only true God, and Jesus Christ, whom you have sent."*
>
> [John 17:1–3]

> - In Jesus' prayer he says that eternal life is found in "knowing God" and in "knowing Jesus". How can we actually know God and Jesus?
> - Jesus spoke of His upcoming crucifixion as being His "glorification". In what way can crucifixion glorify Jesus?

In these words, we see that eternal life is not something for our future. Rather, our eternal life begins now, at the moment of salvation, when our sins are forgiven and we are reconciled to the Father. What awesome truths! To know that we can not only have the promise of eternal life in Jesus Christ but that we can have our sins, which stand between us and God, wiped away by believing in His Son, Jesus Christ as our Lord and Savior.

John seems to have been privy to the content of Jesus' prayers. He (along with his brother James and Simon Peter) was a member of Jesus' innermost circle of disciples. It is probably through this relationship that John had details of Jesus' great prayer.

After his prayer, Jesus left the upper room in central Jerusalem with his disciples and walked about a mile through a gate in the city wall, down into the Kidron Valley and up towards the Mount of Olives just east of the city. There he entered the garden of Gethsemane to pray to his father, God, in great spiritual agony before Judas comes to betray him.

Matthew, one of the disciples. describes the setting and recounts Jesus' words to his eleven closest followers.

"My soul is very sorrowful, even to death; remain here, and watch with me." And going a little farther he fell on his face and prayed, saying, *"My Father, if it be possible, let this cup pass from me; nevertheless, not as I will, but as you will."* (Matthew 26:38-40) Jesus would pray two more times as the disciples slept.

[John 17:4–26]

- **How great was Jesus' agony knowing that he would be separated from his father and expect to bear the punishment for the sins of all humanity, past, present and future?**

- **When we are undergoing difficult times, including intense suffering, why is it important that we remember the suffering that Jesus endured prior to being taken prisoner by the temple guard?**

As we continue in John's gospel account, it is here that Judas arrived with a detachment of soldiers and officials from the chief priests and Pharisees.

Jesus asked, *"Who is it that you want?"*

"Jesus of Nazareth," they replied.

"I am he," Jesus said, after which they drew back and fell to the ground.

Once again, Jesus had ascribed to himself the Name of God. In this scene, His antagonists were well enough versed in scripture that they recognized Jesus' claim and actually fell to the ground either from fear or by the sheer power of God's name.

Jesus asked them again whom it was that they sought and once again they replied that they were looking for Jesus of Nazareth.

"I told you that I am he," Jesus answered. *"If you are looking for me, let these men go."*

Then Peter, who happened to be armed with a sword, drew it and cut off the ear of the high priest's servant. Jesus ordered him to put his sword away. Another gospel records that Jesus then healed the servant's severed ear. Jesus was arrested, bound, and brought to Annas, the father-in-law of Caiaphas, the high priest.

[John 18:1–14]

- **What do you believe to be the significance of Jesus willful surrender to the temple guards when His divine power was so obvious?**
- **Peter made a promise he was not prepared to keep. Have you ever made a promise to God that you did not keep? How has that affected you?**

Peter and another disciple followed Jesus and his captors from a safe distance. However, upon arrival at the palace of Annas, the other disciple, being known by the high priest, was allowed to go with Jesus into the high priest's courtyard. (Many Bible scholars believe that John was this unnamed disciple and that John may have had some indirect connections to those in the priesthood through relatives.) Peter waited outside until the other disciple came back, spoke to a girl on duty there, and was able to bring Peter into the courtyard where a crowd had gathered. The girl asked Peter, *"You are not one of this man's disciples, are you?"* Peter responded, *"I am not."* It was cold and people were standing around a fire so Peter joined them to warm himself.

Annas questioned Jesus about his teaching and his disciples.

Jesus replied. *"I have spoken openly to the world, I always taught in the synagogues or at the temple, where all the Jews come together. I said nothing in secret . . . Ask those who heard me. Surely they know what I said."*

An official struck Jesus in the face and rebuked him for the way he answered.

"If I said something wrong" Jesus replied, *"testify as to what was wrong. But if I spoke the truth, why did you strike me?"* After this, Annas sent Jesus bound to Caiaphas the high priest.

While in the courtyard of Annas' palace, as Peter was warming himself by the fire, Peter was asked a second time, *"You are not one of his disciples, are you?"*

Again, he replied, *"I am not."*

Then, a relative of the man whose ear Peter cut off challenged Peter. *"Didn't I see you with him in the olive grove?"* Again Peter denied any knowledge of Jesus and he began to swear and, with an oath, he reinforced his denial. It was at this time that a rooster began to crow. Peter was reminded of Jesus' words about Peter denying any knowledge of him. Another gospel records that Peter was instantly filled with guilt and remorse for having denied Jesus in His hour of need, so much so that he "went out and wept bitterly". (Matthew 26:75)

[John 18:15–26]

FOR FURTHER DISCUSSION OR PERSONAL REFLECTION:

[JOHN 17:1-26]

In his prayer of John 17, what reason did Jesus give for Judas' betrayal?

According to Jesus' prayer in John 17 what is eternal life?

Why did Jesus pray that His disciples not be taken out of the world? Wouldn't it be easier for believers if they were "taken out of the world"?

How does it make you feel that Jesus prayed for you before you were even born?

[JOHN 18:15-26]

If you could ask Peter how he felt when he heard the rooster crow, what do you think he would tell you? Have you ever felt that way? Why?

SESSION 11

WHY DID JESUS HAVE TO DIE?

John 18:1–19:42

The Garden of Gethsemane was an olive grove located on the slopes of the Mount of Olives and was a familiar place to Jesus and the disciples. When they visited Jerusalem for one of the Jewish holy days, they often went to Gethsemane to escape the crowds of people within the walled city. On this night, the night that Jesus was to be betrayed, Jesus took His disciples with him to this olive grove. It was here that Jesus again prayed, this time asking the Father if there was any other way for His purpose to be completed. It was also here that we gain a glimpse into the struggle between Jesus' humanity and his divinity.

O f the four gospels, John is the only one to exclude this suffering of Jesus' soul from the record. Some find this absence from the record odd since John gives us such a great picture of the duality of "fully God and fully man" in the rest of his gospel account. But the other writers of the gospels do record Jesus suffering as he was under such emotional and spiritual stress that, Luke records, "His sweat was like great drops of blood falling to the ground." (Luke 22:44)

This record is literal and not figurative as some suppose. The phenomenon of "hematidrosis" can occur during times of intense emotional trauma when the dilation of blood vessels pressing against the sweat glands causes the vessels to burst, allowing the blood to seep through the sweat glands and out through the pores of the skin. This gives us a clear indication of the intensity of the struggle occurring inside Jesus on this night.

In the early morning, they led Jesus from Caiaphas to the palace of Pilate, the Roman governor. At this point, Jesus had already been severely beaten by the temple guards, once while on the road from Gethsemane to the palace of Annas, again while he was in the palace, and a third time on the trip to the home of Caiaphas. He must have been less than an impressive sight when he was first seen by Pilate.

The governor came out and asked, *"What charges are you bringing against this man?"* When they told him that Jesus was a criminal, Pilate told the accusers to judge him by their own law – the Jewish rather than the Roman law. They responded that they had no right to execute anyone. Pilate had Jesus brought in and asked him, *"Are you the king of the Jews?"* Jesus asked Pilate where his question came from. Pilate responded with another question. *"What is it that you have done?"*

Jesus replied, *"My kingdom is not of this world. If it were, my servants would fight to prevent my arrest by the Jewish leaders."*

"You are a king, then!" said Pilate.

Jesus answered, *"You say that I am a king. In fact, the reason I was born and came into the world is to testify to the truth. Everyone on the side of truth listens to me."*

Pilate responded with his famous question, *"What is truth?"*

We really have no way of knowing but some believe that it was this ironic question would haunt Pilate for the rest of his time on earth. Pilate was a military man but, since he was chosen to be a governor, he must also have been well educated including studies in the ancient Greek philosophers. The concept of absolute truth had been a subject of debate among the educated elite for centuries and continues to be debated today.

How tragic it was that Pilate still wrestled with this question even as the embodiment of truth stood before him clothed in flesh.

Pilate then returned to the Jews and reported that he found no basis for a charge against Jesus. He reminded them of the custom to release a prisoner at Passover time and offered to release "the king of the Jews." John tells us that, They shouted back, *"No, not him! Give us Barabbas!"* Barabbas had taken part in a rebellion.

[John 18:1-40]

- Pilate asked, *"What is truth?"* (John 18:38) What is your answer to this profound question?

- Jesus told Pilate, *"My kingdom is not of this world"*. (John 18:36) What did He mean by that?

"Then Pilate took Jesus and had him flogged." This statement appears so benign but it fails to translate the immense torture of the "flogging" or "scourging". The whip used in a Roman scourging was also known, in some ancient historical writings, as a "cat-o-nine-tails". It was made from several whips braided together, each having rolled into them chips of jagged stones, bits of sharp metal. With every stroke of the whip, more muscle and bone would have been exposed. It was an evil device intended to mete out stiff punishment for those who were forced to endure its wrath. The victim of the scourging then had both hands tied to a whipping post so that his movement was restricted as much as possible. So severe was the trauma inflicted upon the victim that many sentenced to the scourging post did not survive the beating.

John tells us that after Jesus' scourging, "Soldiers twisted together a crown of thorns and put it on his head. They clothed him in a purple robe and went up to him again and again, saying, *"Hail, king of the Jews!"* And they struck him in the face.

Pilate seemed a bit ambivalent about concurring with Jesus' accusers. *"Look,"* he said to them, *"I am bringing him to you to let you know that I find no basis for a charge against him."* When Jesus came out wearing the crown of thorns and the purple robe, Pilate said to them, *"Here is the man!"*

When they saw Jesus, the chief priests and their officials shouted, *"Crucify! Crucify!"* Pilate gave in and said, *"You take him and crucify him. As for me, I find no basis for a charge against him."* The accusers responded that according to Jewish law he committed blasphemy and had to be executed.

Pilate faced a major dilemma and went back inside his palace and asked Jesus where he was from. Jesus did not reply. Pilate was irritated by Jesus' silence and asked, *"Don't you realize I have power either to free you or to crucify you?"*

Jesus told Pilate, *"You would have no power over me if it were not given to you from above."* He added that those who had handed him over to Pilate were guilty of a greater sin.

From then on, John tells us, Pilate tried to set Jesus free. However, Jesus' accusers knew how to get what they wanted.

"If you let this man go, you are no friend of Caesar," they shouted, *"Anyone who claims to be a king opposes Caesar."*

That challenge, which threatened Pilate's political position, worked. Pilate made one last attempt to avoid responsibility. *"Here is your king,"* he said. *"Shall I crucify your king?"*

The chief priests answered, *"We have no king but Caesar."* So Pilate handed Jesus over to them to be crucified.

[John 19:1–16]

- In the eyes of the Jewish leader, of what was Jesus guilty that merited the death penalty?
- Up to this point in the account of events leading to Jesus' crucifixion, have you seen anyone express any real courage? If so, whom and how?

This exchange, in which the chief priests stated that they had *"no king but Caesar"* demonstrates the lengths to which the Jews would go in order to have Jesus killed. While certain political arrangements between the Roman and Jewish leadership made life for the Jewish leaders much more tolerable than for the average Jew, they still chafed under the rule of a

Gentile kingdom. Roman soldiers having access to the temple mount was especially irritating. Their feelings for the Romans were nothing short of hatred. However, this hatred for the Romans was not as strong as their hatred for Jesus. Their hatred was so powerful that it would cause them to speak the unspeakable as they confessed Caesar, a man who had declared himself to be a god, as their only king.

"Were you there when they crucified my Lord?" is an American spiritual believed to have been written by enslaved African Americans in the 19th century. It calls us to empathize with Christ as the Romans prepared him for crucifixion on Golgotha. Here are the events that unfolded there.

- Four soldiers took charge of Jesus. They made him carry his own cross to what, in the commonly spoken Aramaic language of Jesus and his disciples, was called Golgotha meaning the Place of the Skull.

- Jesus was nailed to and hoisted on his cross between two criminals who were being crucified on that day.

- Pilate had a sign affixed to Jesus' cross that read *"JESUS OF NAZARETH, THE KING OF THE JEWS"*. John tells us that it was written in Aramaic, Latin, and Greek.

- The chief priests protested and said that he should have made the sign read that Jesus *claimed to be* the king of the Jews. Pilate answered, *"What I have written, I have written."*

- The soldiers divided Jesus' garments among themselves as foretold in Psalm 22.

- Jesus' mother, his mother's sister, Mary, the wife of Clopas, and Mary Magdalene stood near the cross. (In John's Gospel, Mary, the mother of Jesus, is mentioned only once and is not mentioned in the other three Gospels. It is evident from what follows that John may have had a personal interest in including Mary.)

- Jesus saw his mother and the disciple "whom he loved" and said, *"Dear woman, here is your son,"* and to the disciple, *"Here is your mother."* From that time on, this disciple took her into his home."

- Jesus said that he was thirsty. They soaked a sponge in wine and vinegar, put it on a stalk of the hyssop plant, and lifted it to his lips.

- When Jesus received the drink, he said, *"It is finished."* With that, he bowed his head and gave up his spirit.

[John 19:17-30]

> Why do you believe the Romans used crucifixion as a means of execution when there were so many other forms of execution that would require much less work?

Since this was unfolding on the Day of Preparation for the Passover, the Jewish leaders asked Pilate to have the legs of those crucified broken, hastening their death and preventing their bodies from being on the crosses on the Sabbath. Victims of crucifixion sometimes lived for many hours or even two or three days so the breaking of the legs of those crucified was not unusual. John records that the soldiers broke the legs of the two thieves who were crucified with Jesus but when they came to Jesus, they found that He was already dead.

Knowing that it was unusual for the condemned man to die this quickly, a soldier was ordered to thrust his spear into Jesus' side. This was done and as the sword tip was pulled out, there was a sudden, copious flow of blood mixed with water. Many modern medical professionals believe that this flow of blood and water was a result of death due to hypovolemic shock, in which fluids fill the membranous sac that surrounds the heart and lungs. This condition was not known to be a common result of crucifixion, especially since it happened within hours of Jesus' execution. But, as John points out, the fact that Jesus' legs were not broken and that he was pierced with a spear happened as a fulfillment of prophecies given hundreds of years prior to the event.

[John 19:31–37]

> On several occasions, John describes an event as one that occurred to "fulfill a prophecy". Why do you believe that he did this?

Chapter 19 ends with Joseph of Arimathea requesting of Pilate that he be allowed to take the body of Jesus from the cross himself. Permission was granted. Jesus' body was rapidly, but only partially, prepared for burial in Joseph's own tomb (another fulfillment of prophecy) and Jesus was placed for his very short stay in the borrowed tomb of a righteous man.

Thus, the human life of God incarnate, one who was born through a miracle and who lived a life marked with miraculous signs and miraculous love, came to an end. It is no wonder that his followers were devastated and confused. The devastation, fear, and confusion were soon to be replaced by joy, wonder, and faith.

[John 19:38–42]

FOR FURTHER DISCUSSION OR PERSONAL REFLECTION:

[JOHN 19:1-9]
If Pilate wanted to set Jesus free, what prevented him from doing so?

[JOHN 19:12]
Jesus' accusers were clever. Bringing the Roman Emperor Caesar into the conversation shifted the dynamics to another level. Why?

[JOHN 19:30]
What do Jesus' words *"It is finished"* mean?

[JOHN 1-19]
You have been on a journey with Jesus and his disciples. Do you sense any change in yourself as a result of your journey? If so, what?

SESSION 12

HOW DID JESUS' CLOSEST FOLLOWERS REACT TO THE RESURRECTION?

John 20:1-31

Another of the gospels records the lengths to which the Jews had gone to prevent any claim by Jesus' followers that he had risen from the dead. They implored Pilate to avoid this possibility by "sealing" the tomb and by posting a guard for three days. The sealing of the tomb entailed securing the large stone covering the entrance to the tomb with strong rope and then affixing the rope to the stone with a wax seal bearing the mark of the Roman Empire. To break such a seal was punishable by death.

Early on, Sunday, the first day of the week, while it was still dark, Mary Magdalene went to the tomb and saw that the stone had been removed from the entrance. She ran to Simon Peter and the other disciple, "the one Jesus loved," (generally understood to be John) and told them that Jesus' body was gone from the tomb. The two disciples ran to the tomb to see this for themselves. When they got there they entered the tomb and found the burial linens and cloth but no Jesus. "The cloth was still lying in its place, separate from the linen," John observed, but neither he nor Peter understood from Scripture what it meant for Jesus to be resurrected from the dead.

[John 20:1-9]

- Why were the Jewish leaders so concerned about the sealing of the tomb and the securing of Jesus' body?
- The gospels record that Jesus arose on "the first day of the week". What significance does this hold for us today?

The disciples returned to their homes, but Mary Magdalene stayed near the tomb weeping. Two angels in white asked her why she was crying. She said it was because they had taken her Lord away and she didn't know where they put him. At this, she turned around and saw Jesus standing there, but she did not realize that it was Jesus.

"Woman," he said, *"why are you crying? Who is it you are looking for?"*

Mary thought it was the gardener and asked him where they had taken Jesus. It was then that the risen Christ spoke Mary's name. She instantly recognized His voice.

She turned toward him and cried out in Aramaic, *"Rabboni!"* (which means Teacher). Jesus told her not to hold onto him because he had not yet gone to the Father. He told her to go tell his brothers (other translations use the term "brethren" that was used in the early church for the Christian community) that he was returning to his Father and their Father, to his God and their God.

Mary went to deliver this news. *"I have seen the Lord!"* she exclaimed, and reported her experience.

[John 20:10–18]

> The Bible states that Mary did not recognize Jesus until He spoke her name. Have you ever felt that you heard Jesus speak your name? If so, what effect did it have on you?

As the disciples gathered behind locked doors because of their fear of the Jews, Jesus came and stood among them and said, *"Peace be with you!"* After he said this, he showed them his hands and side.

It is an understatement to say that the disciples were overjoyed when they saw the risen Christ. Again Jesus said, *"Peace be with you! As the Father has sent me, I am sending you."*

With that Jesus breathed on them and said, *"Receive the Holy Spirit. If you forgive anyone his sins, they are forgiven, if you do not forgive them, they are not forgiven."*

[John 20:19–23]

> Previously we have seen the religious leaders remind Jesus that only God could forgive sins. What has changed?

On this first visitation following Christ's resurrection, only ten of the original twelve were present. Judas, who had betrayed his Lord, had committed suicide. For some reason, Thomas was not present at this meeting, and when the others found him, they said, *"We have seen the Lord."* Thomas responded that unless he saw and touched the nail marks and put his hand into Jesus' side, he would not believe the story of the other disciples. Thomas's response has earned him the nickname "doubting Thomas."

A week later, the disciples were together again. This time Thomas was present. John records that the doors were locked but Jesus came and stood among them and said, *"Peace be with you."*

Then he said to Thomas, *"Put your finger here; see my hands. Reach out your hand and put it into my side. Stop doubting and believe."*

Thomas said to him, *"My Lord and my God!"*

Jesus acknowledged Thomas' belief but added, *"Blessed are those who have not seen and yet have believed."*

[John 19:31–37]

> - **On these three occasions of Jesus appearing to his disciples after his resurrection, He greets them with the words, *"Peace be unto you"*. (John 20:19) What is the significance of this greeting?**
> - **If you were in Thomas' position, do you think that you would have believed the disciples' report without seeing for yourself?**

John reports that Jesus did other miraculous signs in the presence of the disciples not included in his Gospel. "But these are written that you may believe that Jesus is the Christ, the Son of God, and that by believing you may have life in his name."

[John 20:30–31]

FOR FURTHER DISCUSSION OR PERSONAL REFLECTION:

[JOHN 20:1-3]
What do you think happened to Simon Peter that brought him back to the community of the disciples after he had denied knowing Jesus three times?

[JOHN 20:9]
How do you account for John's comment that Peter and he did not yet understand what it meant for Jesus to be resurrected from the dead?

[JOHN 20:24-29]
Thomas, the honest skeptic, had a problem accepting his colleagues' testimony that they had seen the risen Jesus. How should Christians deal with honest skeptics?

[JOHN 20:1-31]
What changes do you see in the disciples as they experience these first encounters with Jesus following his resurrection?

SESSION 13

WHAT DOES TRANSFORMATION LOOK LIKE?

John 21

There is, perhaps, no more relevant chapter in the Bible for the modern believer than the twenty-first chapter of John. Most of us have felt like failures at some point in time. Jesus' treatment of Peter on the shores of the Sea of Galilee offers great hope for those of us who have, at times, made a mess of our lives and even deny that we are followers of Jesus, i.e. we remain silent when we should have spoken up, or gone along with the culture when we should have stood firm in our faith.

John records that sometime after the disciples encounter with Jesus in a room in Jerusalem, some, along with Peter, had returned to the shores of the Sea Galilee. There Peter declared, *"I am going fishing."* This was more than a statement of intent and Peter's fishing trip was not for recreation. Peter, having failed Jesus when he denied Christ in his greatest hour of need, still felt the paralyzing sting of a complete but unexpected failure. Peter's fishing trip was a sign of giving up. In spite of Jesus' words indicating that Peter would be a great leader in spreading the good news of Christ, Peter intended to return to a life with which he was familiar. He was a fisherman prior to meeting Jesus. He could be a fisherman again. It is in this state of mind that Peter revisited the shores of the Sea of Galilee. One of the great tragedies of his decision is that several of the other disciples followed him into this return to the familiar, an act that was contrary to Jesus' plans for their lives.

[John 21:1–3]

> - Have you ever suffered a significant failure in your walk with Christ? If so, how did it make you feel and how did you renew your relationship with Christ?
> - Do you believe that your decisions regarding your faith affect the spiritual lives of other believers?

In spite of all this, Peter and some of the other disciples went fishing for one whole night. They caught nothing. Early the next morning, they heard a voice calling from the shore, *"Friends, haven't you any fish?"*

"No," they replied.

He said, *"Throw your net on the right side of the boat and you will find some."*

When they did this, the net was so full of fish that they could not haul it in. This scene must have brought back memories for several of them since it was in this manner that they had first met Jesus.

Then the disciple whom Jesus loved said to Peter, *"It is the Lord."* When he heard those words, Peter didn't wait until the boat was pulled onto shore, he jumped into the water and headed to the beach. The other disciples soon followed bringing the boat with its net full of fish to the shore. There they saw a fire of burning coals with fish on it and some bread. Jesus asked them to bring some of the fish they had just caught and invited them to breakfast. From the scriptures recording this event, it appears that the disciples did not recognize Jesus or, perhaps, thought they were seeing an apparition. No other explanation is given as to why they would not ask Him *"Who are you?"*

[John 21:3–14]

> ▪ **Why do you believe that the disciples did not always recognize Jesus in His resurrected form?**

After breakfast, Jesus did something quite symbolic. He asked Peter if he truly loved him.

"Yes," Peter responded, *"you know that I love you."*

Jesus then said, *"Feed my lambs."*

Jesus repeated his question to Peter. Peter responded with the same answer.

Jesus said, *"Take care of my sheep."*

A third time, Jesus asked Peter the same question. This time, expressing hurt and frustration, Peter responded, *"Lord you know all things; you know that I love you."*

Jesus said, *"Feed my sheep,"* and, after a few additional comments, said to Peter, *"Follow me!"*

[John 21:15–19]

> - How does this exchange with Peter demonstrate that even when we fail miserably Jesus still loves us and pursues us. How does Jesus help prevent us from being destroyed by our guilt and shame?
> - In what ways does Jesus seek us out?

The encounter with Peter shows us that Jesus meets us where we are and speaks to us in a language that we will understand and to which we will respond. Three times Peter had denied Jesus and three times Jesus gave him the opportunity to proclaim his love for his Lord. As far as Christ was concerned, the matter was settled. Three proclamations of faith following three declarations of denial was not necessary. However, this was something to which Peter could relate. From that time forward, we see Peter being the leader that Jesus had intended for him to be.

John concluded his Gospel by saying that he was the disciple who testified to these things and wrote them down. He added that Jesus did many other things and that, "If every one of them were written down, I suppose that even the whole world would not have room for the books that would be written."

[John 21:20–25]

- How many times do you believe that Jesus will forgive you of a particular sin?

- Have you ever wrestled with a sin for which you seemingly cannot find forgiveness? How have you dealt with it? If you are still dealing with it, how will your understanding of Jesus and the Holy Spirit bring about a satisfactory resolution.

Throughout this study we hope you have observed how John's gospel is unique in many ways. More clearly than any of the other writers, John demonstrates how Jesus transformed a group of men from different walks of life into the vessels that would bear the transforming power of Jesus to the world. As he writes about this transforming power, John explains that once the transformation has begun in a person, that individual will never be the same. Paul, a one-time persecutor of Christians, understood this as well as anyone when, following his encounter with Jesus, wrote

"And I am sure of this, that he who began a good work in you will bring it to completion at the day of Jesus Christ." (Philippians 1:6 ESV)

To know Jesus personally is to really experience Your Transformation.

FOR FURTHER DISCUSSION OR PERSONAL REFLECTION:

[JOHN 1-21]

Having seen how Jesus transformed the lives of the disciples, and the other men and women who followed him, are you willing to let Jesus transform you?

What does this Gospel convey about how you may be spiritually transformed?

Are you willing to let Jesus continually transform you spiritually for the rest of your life?

What steps will you take now to start your transformation? Will you come back and share your plan with the group?

EPILOGUE

During the 13 sessions of this study, you've sampled a bit of what the first disciples experienced as they walked with Jesus through the three and a half years of his active ministry. You've had a whirlwind adventure together with those in your group!

Questions have guided your time of dialog during this study. We'd like to leave you with a few more questions to consider on your own.

1. Are you willing to ask Jesus to give you a new beginning with him and transform your life?

2. Can you make following him your highest priority?

3. What would you tell someone else about what you're learning about Jesus?

4. Are you willing to share the Good News about him with others in your world?

As you continue to journey with Jesus, please remember that you are not traveling alone. He's gone ahead of you to blaze the trail, and he promises to be with you every step of the way. He promises to give a purposeful, flourishing and meaningful life now and for eternity to all who journey with him, to each person who affirms that Jesus is Lord and Savior. Moreover, he has promised to provide the wisdom, the power and even the words you need to invite others to follow him, too.

If you enjoyed this study of the Gospel according to John, You may want to study a different view of the life of Jesus as told by the Apostle Mark. *YOUR INVITATION*, is an 11-session small-group exploration designed to deepen your understanding of God's love and forgiveness as expressed in the life and teachings of Jesus Christ. *YOUR INVITATION*, from Living Dialog Ministries, is available from online retailers and bookstores everywhere.

Please visit our website, www.lifesbasicquestions.com, for a place to engage some of the core questions of life. The website is designed to be a user-friendly way to dialog about the kinds of issues you encountered in your study of the Gospel of Mark. There is also a place on the website for visitors to ask their own questions, and receive a confidential response from the Living Dialog Ministry team. It's a helpful, no-cost resource you can share with others.

ABOUT US

Directors of the Living Dialog Ministries

JOHN C. (JACK) DANNEMILLER, Chairman and CEO of The Living Dialog Ministries, is the former Chair and CEO of Applied Industrial Technologies, a Fortune 1000 corporation. He is a 30-year leader of small group Bible studies, a frequent speaker at Christian Businessmen events, and a lecturer at the Weatherhead Graduate School of Business of Case Western Reserve University where he was honored with the Distinguished Alumni Award.

IRVING R. STUBBS, President and Executive Editor of The Living Dialog Ministries, is a minister with degrees from Davidson College and Union Theological Seminary in New York. He served in pastorates, an urban ministry, and consultant to business, media, religious, government, and professional organizations and their executives in North America, Europe, and Asia. He is the author and co-author of books, articles, and learning resources.

HENRY R. (HARRY) POLLARD, IV, Secretary of The Living Dialog Ministries, is Chairman, Partner, and Practicing Attorney with Parker, Pollard, Wilton & Peaden, PC of Richmond, Virginia where he has practiced law for more than 40 years. He has served as an officer and director of numerous businesses including banking, real estate, and financial entities. He is co-founder and Chairman of The Values Institute of America.

KENT E. ENGELKE, Treasurer of The Living Dialog Ministries, is a Managing Director and Chief Economic Strategist for Capitol Securities Management, a $6.1 billion asset management company, and has served as a director of several publicly traded banks and mortgage banking firms. His views on the economy and the markets are routinely solicited by major media outlets. He credits God for the words he writes daily and thanks God for courage and perseverance in overcoming obstacles.

BRIAN N. REGRUT, Executive Director of The Living Dialog Ministries, is a former public relations executive and consultant, corporate speech writer, author and lecturer serving clients in the fields of telecommunications, financial services and education. He has served in a variety of church leadership roles including preaching and teaching. He and his wife of 51 years have taught Sunday School together and have led small group Bible studies for many years.

A THOUGHT-PROVOKING EVANGELISM TOOL FOR CHURCHES AND ORGANIZATIONS

For those on a journey of discovery, finally answers to the profound questions of life. This little book has been distributed to thousands.

Available in bulk at a reasonable cost with a customized cover featuring your logo and message from your church or organization.

Join the dialog
www.lifesbasicquestions.com

For pricing email
lifesbasicquestions@outlook.com

CHECK OUT OUR OTHER SMALL GROUP EXPLORATIONS

YOUR INVITATION

helps guide small groups in an exciting exploration, through Intentional dialog, of the Gospel of Mark.

Each of the 11 sessions starts with a thought-provoking question that leads the group into a short, biblically-accurate narrative interspersed with questions the group can use as dialog starters.

LIGHTING THE WAY

guides groups through an exploration of the Apostle Paul's letter to the followers of Christ who lived in Rome. In this epistle, Paul lays down the principal doctrines of Christianity that have guided the Church for two millennia.

Each of the 12 sessions starts with a thought-provoking question followed by biblically accurate, narrative interspersed with questions the group can use as dialog starters.

www.ingramcontent.com/pod-product-compliance
Lightning Source LLC
Chambersburg PA
CBHW072058290426
44110CB00014B/1730